# LOVE or LUST

## Antwan Williams

iUniverse, Inc.
New York   Bloomington

LOVE OR LUST

iUniverse books may be ordered through booksellers or by contacting:

iUniverse
1663 Liberty Drive
Bloomington, IN 47403
www.iuniverse.com
1-800-Authors (1-800-288-4677)

ISBN: 978-1-4401-3111-0 (pbk)
ISBN: 978-1-4401-3112-7 (ebk)

Printed in the United States of America

iUniverse rev. date: 4/06/2009

# CONTENTS

# CHAPTER 1:
# THE INTRODUCTION

Where should I begin in this strange world of curiosity? I guess I shall tell you that everything you probably know about love is wrong. I believe in some way the original concept of love has been lost. It has been altered and molded into what we know now as love. Which is the object of some physical part of the body? Or it is measured by the length of one's money. The word love is used so much today, that it has been stripped of its true meaning. Love meant something so much more, but now it's worthless. In transition, there's a way we can get it back. We can make it how it use to be before we attached so many stereotypes to it. We can truly and sincerely love again the way it was suppose to be. Now if you are that few percent that has found love already, than this does not apply to you. Most likely if you are reading this, than that means you are a lost player in the game right now. Therefore, in your case this is directed towards you. First, I will teach you how to distinguish love from lust. Second, I will explain the four color codes of love to you. Third, I will teach you how to find, acquire, and keep love. So without further do, let us begin our journey to the unknown.

# CHAPTER 2:
# WHAT'S LOVE OR LUST

All right now we need to reacquaint ourselves with some common terminology. What is the difference between love and lust? A lot of people get the two confused today. That's because most people today are lusting and they actually believe its love. The reason being is because they both are very similar and carry the same symptoms. Some people think if a few tears is shed that it has to be love. I remember departing from the mother of my child to move to another city. We actually cried and said our goodbyes. The real reason I left is because I knew we really didn't have that sincerity anymore. What we had was not love, we was just comfortable with each other. Most people said its love because we showed a lot of emotions. But all we had was strong emotions, not love. Whenever you lay with a person that is a sacred moment? But we lust so much today, that we confuse making love with having sex. It's really important that you find that small difference because it can alter a whole lifetime. Love is a permanent emotion that last forever. It can't be bargained or sold for materialistic things. It satisfies the heart, which is fed by the soul. Now lust is a temporarily satisfaction that satisfies the physical body. For instance, when you have sex with somebody your in love with or at least look at sincere you know it. Or you may think you know it and it could be an effectuation. But in this case let's say you do know it. The reason being is because after the climax is over you don't mind holding them and starring into their eyes. That means its something sincere you feel for that person. Now try that very same thing with a one night stand or some friend with benefits. After the climax is over look them right in the eyes and say slowly to yourself you love them. If you can't say and mean those sincere words, than you know what you just had was a lustful experience. As a matter of fact after the climax is over you won't even look at them the same. The reason is because you were on a lustful high when you judged them the first time. Watch how unappealing they look to you after that high is gone. Also you wouldn't want to cuddle hug or kiss.

Why you may ask, that's because everything you felt for them was nothing but lust. And remember what I told you, lust is a temporarily satisfaction. Even if the person you're laying next to swears that was love the both of you just made. You know the truth of the matter. It was nothing but a lustful encounter. Why you may ask? Its no way you can be deeply in love with a person if they did not project those sincere feelings towards you. Let me clarify what I mean with this concept. In order for you to really love someone, true sincere emotions must be showed from that person. If not, than what you're experiencing is nothing but an infatuation. A selfish emotion created from your mind to keep you from accepting the reality of the situation. Think about it to yourself for a minute. Remember that stalker you could never get rid of who swears they loved you. Even though, you never showed him anything but common courtesy he was crazy over you. Now it's a difference when you have showed him all these emotions behind close doors, and claim you didn't do anything. That's because you understand what you shared with him was lust, and you apparently want to keep it under wraps. Unfortunately, he believes that all what you have showed him was real. He was experiencing nothing but an infatuation. Consequently, its nothing different from the one night stand you had that wont leave you alone because he's deeply in love with you. I was lusting for a longtime with a close friend of mine who was experiencing the same thing. We were friends with benefits since we first met. Now when I first met her she had a fiancé. We stilled engaged in sexual activity, we kept it on the down low. Over time one thing leads to another and we started hanging out everyday. She eventually got side tracked with me so her fiancé called it quits. Now she always told me how much she likes me and she wanted to be with me. She would frequently say she loves me and tells me that she trust me. I repeatedly told her that what she is feeling is not love, but lust. Within first meeting each other it was nothing but sex, that's it. Not to mention she was still dealing her fiancé and other guys. When we were done she would go back home to him and play her role. I didn't mind because I understood we were nothing but friends, but she would get mad if I talked to other girls. I can't tell you how many times she told me she is not dealing with anyone except for me. I knew she was lying because her phone would ring all night from different guys. So I put her word to the test and sent my friend to get with her behind my back. Now this isn't your common situation where the jerk puts the hopeless girl off to his friends. I am writing a book exploring love and lust, so I need real evidence for real facts. Also any respectable women would not entertain the idea from the back stabbing friend. But in this case I knew she was a luster, I just wanted to have thorough proof. Please understand there must be no pity showed for lusters. They know what they are doing. Lusters want to lust but still be treated like lovers, but there will be no pity spared in this book. Anyways I told my friend to simply tell her he wanted to have sex with her. I had been studying her so I knew she would with out a doubt get in the car. Sure enough they hopped in his car and drove to the same spot we parked at for some midnight sex. I was actually parked around the corner in my car watching from a distance. He said his pants were down and everything was going as plan, but he couldn't get it up. They drove off and departed on their way to their homes. Understand that even though nothing happen, she is still guilty. She still got into his car and parked at a designated area. She was guilty the minute she got into his car. Now plenty of time went pass until I said anything about that situation. Consequently, day after day she told me that she loves me and is committed to me and only me. So one day I told her I would be with her if she was completely honest with me. Even though I knew I would never really get with her knowing her true identity, I wanted to see if she would tell the truth. I asked her was there anything I needed to know, about any past acts that can potentially harm us in the future. In a blink of an eye she responded with a quick no. I asked her over and over is she sure about her answer? She kept telling me she has nothing to hide from me. I bagged back from the car and looked her straight in the eyes. I told her she has one more chance to come clean about anything that I need to know, anything involving a friend of mine. She instantly started crying heavily as her face turned cherry red. She repeatedly stated nothing happen and kept defending herself. I told her if nothing happen, than why is she crying. She kept making up sad excuses to why she was so emotional. I told her now she understands why I can't be with her. Than a couple of weeks later she was promising and swearing to me, that she isn't sexually involved with no one but me. Again I asked her was she telling the truth, and she stated yes and promised to god. Now what she didn't know is I saw her instant message five minutes earlier on her phone. She was getting out the car and her phone fell on the floor. It was flipped open and I saw the message clear as daylight. The message read, "Thanks for coming over and taking a shower with me". Earlier that day she told me she had a doctor's appointment to go to. Well I guess he checked her out very well before coming to see me.

You will come to find out that there are serious consequences from playing the lusting game. One fact you must always remember about lust, it can only end with hurt. If not both of you, understand one of you will certainly be hurt. It's not made to be a permanent situation. Think about every lustful encounter you ever had. How many of them can you say ended well? How many of them didn't force you to loose someone who was once a friend? You have to know lusting is not for everybody. Some people can't handle such a thing. If you can't control your emotions, than you can't play that game. For example, how many of you knew of that relationship that started off as sex but nothing more. Than after a couple sessions you notice jealousy starts to form. Before you know it, you're fighting with them over a phone call from someone in your past. The truth is most people who say they can handle that lustful relationship really can't. And as harsh as it seems I don't feel sorry for them when they pout about how much it hurts. Those are the chances you take when playing with lust.

# CHAPTER 3:
# HOW TO PIN POINT A DISASTER

I'm also going to show you how to pin point a disaster before it happens. Nine times out of ten we are the cause of our own problems in relationships. Why, because we avoid the obvious wrong turn signals we see at the beginning when we meet a person. Within the first five minutes you should be able to tell if a person is approaching you in a sincere way, or if they are on a lustful high. They should be giving you positive feedback and actually listening. You speaking while there simply agreeing and giving head nods is not conversation. Ask direct questions looking them straight in the eyes. What you're looking for is direct responses. For the ladies, if you catch a man glancing down once or twice that's okay. It's nothing wrong with them admiring your sexual appeal. The problem is when they can't give you any feedback and there looking everywhere else except for in your eyes. For the men, watch if a woman seems to be hitting you hard with heavy materialistic questions. If she's asking about what car you drive and how much you make before knowing your name she is a materialistic luster.   That's the red flag that this is not a sincere person. Also you want to pay close attention to what comes out there mouth while speaking. Understand if there is any talk about sex within a couple of minutes of meeting a person, they are on a lustful high. There is no reason why sex should be brought up that early in the conversation. Now if you are looking for a lustful encounter, than there's your ticket. But if you're looking for someone sincere you're looking for patience. Unfortunately, our generation does not have patience when getting to know people. Today we give in too quick with our sexual desires. I wonder what will happen if we just wait a little. If you can't sit for an hour or two and talk maturely about getting to know each other, it's a waste of time.

I also want to talk about the only level of lusting which is okay. I call this level beginners lust.  Have you ever hit it off real good with somebody on the first date? Than unconsciously you find yourself thinking a little inappropriate about them, even though you know you would never do such a thing so early. Well that is nothing but beginner's lust. That's actually a good sign of strong chemistry. Most people can't buy strong chemistry these days. Just don't make the mistake of being direct with those feelings too early before you can figure the person out. Or you will quickly see your sincere relationship turn into a lustful one. Let me give you a comparison I frequently use. Exploring passion with someone for the first time is like the value of gold. If you give it away to early the value drops and you become like the rest of the peas in the pot. If you give away too much it's not important anymore. It's not scarce so therefore it's not needed. Now it's not called passion anymore, now it's called sex. Now if you hold onto it long enough, over time the value increases. Now it's much valuable and important than ever before. Now it doesn't matter how much you give it away because the bar is set. Try it out next time you're involved, and see how you like the results.

# CHAPTER 4:
# THE COLOR CODES

Now that we have established the difference from love and lust we can get into the color codes. You ever wondered why certain people act different in certain situations toward love. That's because I believe everybody is coded with certain genes and patterns that make them react different. So I took a poll and found out through my statistics, that there are similarities with certain people. I then created four colors for the four different genders. We have white, blue, red, and yellow. Through my research I have found out similarities from all the colors. Understand these color codes are based off of emotions towards love and relationships. This cannot predict a person's personal characteristics such as being selfish or cheap. My studies were based on emotions towards love in relationships, nothing more. I will need you to pay close attention as I take you through this new realm.

# CHAPTER 5:

# THE WHITE COLOR CODE

We will start off with exploring the white color code first. I often refer to the whites as the lone wolves of the pack. I noticed everybody in this code has some sort of independence factor towards love. Whites are more logical thinkers when it comes to love. They are dedicated people when it comes to dealing with emotions. Most of them are not too thrilled about finding that perfect love. In fact some whites go through life living the single and free lifestyle. Sure they engage in relationships but most people let them down. They can come off as the uptight ones or the ones who barely have time. There everyday jobs and hobbies is a substitute for not dealing with love. Most of them come off as being stuck up or high maintenance, but the truth is you really have to show and prove to them you love them. Most whites just simply do not want to invest the time it takes to find love. Many have been let down and do not enjoy the feeling of being heartbroken. Also they can get bored really fast with most people. It is not easy to convince them that you are a sincere person. Also the ones who do let you close will often take it slow. They are really good at observing and critiquing one's character. The good thing about them is they are loyal people when dealing with emotions. They don't like taking the easy way out and would rather struggle before giving up on their spouse. Every color approaches and deals with love in a different way. Whites don't make decisions based off their emotions. They will make the most logical decision before relying on their heart. Dreams and fairytales of love don't strike them too strong as it would another color. Whites are usually not the first to stick their neck out for love. You have to take the first step with them. You have to be patient with them and show them true love. I actually had a chance to acquire a white, but I messed it up. She was a woman so beautiful that she created butterflies in my stomach every time I heard her voice. Now understand when I say beautiful I'm not just talking about physically. Her personality was beautiful to me also, and I frequently found myself grabbing for words to say when talking to her. Sad to say I was unstable at the time and I didn't keep the previous date we arranged. I just dropped off at the end of the earth somewhere. The real reason I backed off was I actually was down and out of money. I didn't know how to simply tell her I wouldn't be able to take her out. I thought I would look like a disgrace so I just avoided it. I thought a woman of her caliber did not have to deal with such weakness. So I guess I don't have to tell you she didn't respond to positive to that. I can say she was more beautiful than life itself, but you already know that Siyo. See whites have the potential of being the most loyalist lovers of all time. Consequently, if you happen to betray them you may not get a second chance. Whites are very strict and serious when it comes to there feelings. You only get one time to screw them over. Love them and they will stand by your side forever. In transition, if you hurt them it's your lost.

# CHAPTER 6:

# THE BLUE COLOR CODE

Moving on lets see if you can keep up with the blue color code. This color code is referred to as the lovers. If ever you were looking for a sincere and romantic person, you will find it in the blues. They are said to be the true lovers of the galaxy. They react, move, and live off their emotions. The only problem is this gender is very low in population and is dieing out. I believe it has something to do with people not approaching love accurately. Blues have the ability to sharply distinguish from love and lust. And they can very well spot a lustful relationship from a far. They tend to want that real natural love, that which you see in the movies. They can have a temporarily lustful relationship too. We are all creatures of habit, so it's not unnatural for us to have sexual urges. Consequently, the blues can't dwell within lust too long. Lust only satisfies the physical body not the soul. Therefore, blues will separate from that situation, being that their raw nature is love. Yes it's possible for them to lust occasionally also, but they will not be satisfied from it. Blue's stay continually looking for sincere relationships leading towards love. Other color codes don't have the ability to pursue love so strongly like this one. Blues approach love aggressive and will give all they have. They will sacrifice everything, if it's a possibility to have true love. The problem is when they try so hard, they take the risk of falling so hard. Other color codes don't welcome this process. For instance, the white color code does not agree with the concept of sacrificing for love. Reason being the whites don't possess the desire for love as strongly as the blues. Therefore, they could never recuperate as fast or as strong as a blue can from heartbreak. Blues are exceptionally unique when it comes to love, but they have a downside as does every color. If a blue is constantly hurt in a repeated amount of consecutive attempts while chasing love. They can go into what I call a dark zone, where they will temporarily forfeit from love to gather themselves. Some will lye dormant or alone and others may play the lusting game for sometime. Sooner or later they will pull themselves together and step back into their nature. So if true love is what you seek, than go find yourself a blue. The only problem is you have a 1 in 10 percent chance of finding one.

# CHAPTER 7:
# THE RED COLOR CODE

So now we can get into the red color code, which I often refer to as the defiant ones. That's because most reds don't agree with the concept and rules of love. They prefer to approach love in their own way. This can be a good thing because it allows reds to be creative and enthusiastic. Also, it can be a bad thing because it breaks all rules of following any organized method. Most reds will often at times settle for a lustful relationship. Now when I say lustful I don't mean it in just a sexual form like I've used earlier. A lustful relationship can appear in many ways besides sex. It's also a relationship where two people remain together, knowing their not serious and sincere about each other. For instance, when I was with the mother of my child, I knew that we weren't in love with each other and yet I stayed with her. I knew we were not being sincere with each other and she knew it too. Consequently, we were still holding on, even though we knew we had given up in our minds. Therefore, what we had was a lustful relationship. Any time you endure a relationship without your heart truly in it, it is therefore a lustful relationship. Most reds share that trait for settling for something average. The reason they settle because most of them have never experienced real love. Therefore, it's hard for them to pinpoint it when they see it. For example, the whites know how to approach love but usually won't approach it first. The reds will approach love but usually in the wrong way. In transition, they get frustrated easily and will give up on love if it seems too complicated. Now understand I said they will give up on love not on their spouse. Meaning they won't pay attention to those sincere emotions and will simply take they heart out of it. At the same time they will cater to the relationship while they seek a way out. Unconsciously they will create their own version of love with their rules. They will deal with an easy situation, before struggling with the wrath of love. Reds can be very unorthodox when dealing with their emotions. Reds find it very hard confining to another and committing to them. The reason being is because reds tend to hold their pride high above them. In fact there pride will usually keep them from acquiring love. Reds are afraid of getting hurt and being let down. They feel vulnerable with their guards are let down and exposed. Another problem is they can't control their emotions when hurt. They tend to make irrational decisions when emotions flare up. Reds must be shown how to spot love and direct their emotions. It will most likely take a blue to show them true love. The good thing is reds are determined and vigorous once they experience true love. They have the ability to be one of the most intriguing lovers. They love the feeling of being wanted and cared for. The thing is will they let go and risk it all, will they sacrifice everything for love. Can you make them see the value of true love? Most of them don't know the ways of love simply because they don't try. For most reds you must show them how to love by the rule book. The trick is, are you strong enough to do such a thing.

# CHAPTER 8:
# THE YELLOW COLOR CODE

The last color code of the group is the infamous yellows. This is one of the most unorthodox colors of the four. This color brakes up into two separate categories. One of two is called the lusters and the other is called the peacekeepers. Both carry some of the same traits such as being over emotional and exaggerate. In transition, they are two entirely different breeds. We will start with the luster's which is the majority of the two. In fact there are more luster's walking around than any other color codes. Lusters are strictly driven by sexual needs. They are satisfied by lustful encounters and sexual things only. In fact, lusters cannot see and understand love like any other color code. They interpret everything based on a sexual level, or they base everything on materialistic things. Materialistic lusters are so blinded by the worldly riches, that materialistic things are a climax for them. It immobilizes them from ever seeing a person for who they really are. Most of them have picked up the term gold digger. Sexual luster's are some of the men you refer to as dogs or the women you would call a slut. They will pretty much do anything to satisfy that sexual urge, even if it means crossing a love one. Consequently, most lusters actually know how to pin point love. The problem is their fast paced emotions and high drive for excitement does not agree with love's chemical make up. Most of them want to be in love and experience true sincere feelings. They don't have the patience to play by the rules, due to their strong focus on sexual tension and materialistic things. Luster's usually float through life carefree in and out of lustful relationships. Having a different spouse every other day or a week is normal to them. They are good when it comes to role playing and trying to tempt others into believing there sincere. So many lusters portray themselves to be blues so often, they have tainted real lovers. The playing field has become so intense today with approaching others, that most lovers are mistaken for lusters. You must be strict on body language and eye contact when revealing a luster. Give them the image of a sincere individual and give no attention to any lustful words or acts. If they bring up anything on a sexual level shut them down immediately. Give them no room to stretch or joke with any sexual comment. Keep this up as long as you can and you will see a couple of changes. First, they will either slack off you a little and the phone calls will start to fade. This is a sign of a luster getting tired of the waiting game. The focus of attention is dropping due to no sexual activity. Or you will notice a high increase in the chemistry level between the both of you. Meaning the opposite attraction is not a luster and is pursuing you seriously. Understand there are some luster's that will go the distance to achieve that sexual climate. They will cater to you with materialistic things and flattering words. This method will expose them if you don't let up. But most of the time we do, and than we claim we couldn't see the disaster coming. There is tons of luster's walking around scouting new recruits to pray on everyday. Understand most of them are not meant to find love. They are totally fine with multiple sexual encounters that often result in brutal break ups. Most of the male lusters will usually put up a fight when exposed. They will constantly swear and stay in denial about cheating. Some of the females will use crying when exposed as a method to rekindle the flame. Understand all lusters will lie to the very last extent to remain out of the radar. They use and abuse as many chances as you give them. In a strange way they really can't help it. Maybe it's because it's all they know. So if you play the lusting game with them, understand it all ends in hurt.

Now that we have finished the first category of the yellow color lets get started on the next category in the infamous yellows. This next breed of the yellow color code is the peacekeepers. Peacekeepers are a very interesting and unbalance breed of players. They are very emotional beings and they usually where they heart on their sleeve. The reason is because peacekeepers can't control or measure their emotions. It's similar to running a pressing machine without an on or off switch. Most of them apply to much energy at the wrong time. Some of them apply too little at the wrong time. They find it difficult and confusing when dealing with hurtful situations. For instance, a white gender will not be drastically affected by heartbreak or disappointment. That's because most whites know how to control and level their emotions. Peacekeepers emotions are to unstable and inconsistent to be leveled. Some are very over emotional in every situation, others can occasionally exaggerate and over react. This is the category where you will find some of your stalkers and deranged spouses. Their emotions can get away from them sometimes. They carry a big heart, which usually results in them giving more emotionally than their spouse. This can be a good thing and also a bad thing. It's a good trait because it displays a loving and affectionate person. Consequently, giving too much can show signs of an over emotional lover. Peacekeepers can't mingle in and out of deep relationships like others. They can't bounce back as quick from heartbreak like others. There emotions are too sensitive for such a thing. The positive thing is they have the ability to look for the good in everybody. They love to cater to emotions and also be catered to. Most of the time, others take their kindness for weakness. Overall, peacekeepers are warm and accepting people in relationships. They sometimes approach love at the wrong pace. The only problem is finding someone with the patience to deal with their uncontrollable and unpredictable emotions.

I have actually dealt with one and it can be a roller coaster ride. It was actually my fought because I already knew how unstable her emotions were, but I still dealt with her. We went through a lot of ups and downs from miscommunications over our emotions. She was ready for a relationship and I wasn't. However in some form of way I lead her on. I should not have let certain things happen, knowing I wasn't ready to commit to her. Even though she kept saying she could handle it, I knew she couldn't. Understand whenever you are in a situation where you have more control, the responsibility is on you. But when you hang around close with someone for so long, people start to grow on you. That's actually how some people in up in relationships where they remain unhappy. They got in too far where it's hard to comeback without deeply hurting the other. So instead they choose to settle, and later they start to believe that there meant for each other. Unfortunately when people get caught up in that storm, they can no longer see what's really out there for them. But I knew I couldn't let it go that far. So we ended up getting into multiple arguments, due to us being on different levels emotionally. She actually stood by my side and befriended me and I thank her for that. Consequently, I want to confess something to her that she doesn't know about. I'll talk in first person because I know your reading this. Remember we kept arguing about you giving too much and being too eager to please me. You always use to buy me things and go out of your way. I told you I would prefer you to stop doing so much because I didn't want you to complain when upset. You repeatedly told me its okay, because you do not give with strings attached. I told you I been through that before, where someone has threw it back in my face. You stated you are not like everyone else. Well I happen to over here a certain someone talking with someone else, and they were talking about us. They talked about how you told them that you felt I was inconsiderate. That I and my family were using you, and I'm taking advantage of you. I thought at first that maybe these two did not know what they were talking about. They started talking about private things, which only you knew about. Things that I know never left my mouth so it had to leave yours. I never told you about this because I didn't think it was the right time. But I think now is the perfect time to inform you that I know what was discussed. You hate so much when I compare you to other girls, but you behaved that same way they did. It's still okay though because you still were there for me. I just wanted you to read this, and when you finish sit back and smile.

# CHAPTER 9:
# THE HYBRID COLORS

Through my studies I encountered several occasions where I had an extremely difficult time placing some people. I noticed some individuals answered keenly to one color, but also answered keenly to another color. I also noticed most of them were slightly confused on there answers. They fought with them selves in a confusing way while trying to figure themselves out. The reason was because they were having mixed fillings about two opposite answers. They felt one way about something, than after a couple minutes they felt the exact opposite. Mix breeds are very unpredictable people which make them spontaneous. Consequently, it can also make them unreliable in some situations of not knowing what part of them you're going to get. Most likely there is a very small chance you will run into one of them. You have a higher chance in meeting a blue, even though that's nearly impossible also.

# CHAPTER 10:
# IS IT POSSIBLE TO CHANGE COLORS

The question of change is by far the most frequently asked questions from all my volunteers. It is possible for some people to change colors, but it's a very slim possibility that most will. See most people say they want to change when upset, angry, or disappointed. The problem is once they calm down; they go back to their raw and original habits. I call this spontaneous unstable emotion temperamental anger. This is usually what most people feel when they say they're going to change. I found out its possible to change from serious and life threatening situations. It can be a situation that's breaks or triggers emotions to their boiling point. An example would be the sudden death of a spouse. This event has been known to change some people color codes, and some others still remain the same. In transition, the majority of people make themselves believe they have changed when they never do.

# CHAPTER 11:

# ACCEPT WHO YOU ARE

Now that you understand the color codes lets start our journey to finding love. Before anything can be achieved you must first accept yourself for who you really are. Understand this process is based on the information you give. If what you're stating about yourself is not true, it's no way to find your true color. I can't tell you the countless volunteers who answered the questions based on who they want to be, instead of who they are. These people never find they true color because they won't accept who they really are. Be honest with what you like and what you would prefer in your spouse. If you tend to judge people by the physical body alone, than you may very well be a luster. It's nothing wrong with lusting if you can handle such a thing. It's better than receiving false information which you know does not apply to you. Unfortunately, if you are a luster you would most likely end up lying to yourself about being a luster. Remember most luster's are in denial about their selves. I'll give you a common example of what I mean. I went out on a date with a friend of a friend. We drove around town and talked for hours about everything except for sex. We talked about family, careers, and marriage. There was no sexual signs or conversations brought up. Now when we arrived at my place we parked outside and continued talking. I brought up a conversation on sex to see her reaction. She gave me feedback heavily and even went further into detail with favorite positions. That was a small clue to unraveling her code, but I couldn't base her being a luster on just a small conversation of sex. So I went further and further making sure our number one topic was sex. Just like I thought she went right into it with me showing signs of being aroused. When departing I went in for a kiss and things got passionate. In fact, she even gave me some oral pleasure in the car. We left on the note that we were going to continue the next day. Once inside my house I knew very well I just encountered a luster despising herself as a lover. Although I already knew she was a luster before I got involved with her, I had to make sure. For real facts you need real life situations. What I didn't tell you was I previously crept up on her at the club and observed her from a distance. She was heavily flirting with almost every guy in the club. In fact, she even kissed several of them and gave her number to them also. It seemed as though she was a rollercoaster and everybody was taking their turn. I knew I had to put my theory to the test with raw evidence. This is too big of a thing to just base it off of a hunch. So that's how we ended up in the car. Now what I really wanted you to pick up on is how she presented a false image to me. In the car she told me how respectful she is and how picky she is with men. Earlier in the club she scouted out men like skittles and it seemed as though everyone got a taste of the rainbow. She also told me she is looking for a sincere guy to be her man. She displayed to me all the signs and characteristics a man would want in a woman. I observed her body language and conversation carefully. I caught some things the average person would have probably over looked. She told me she falls for the married guys even though she's aware of there situation. That right there told me she is not a sincere individual in relationships. Why would you constantly cater to men who are already involved with someone else? That means she consciously goes into these relations with them accepting they will never truly be with her. That can only mean the satisfaction she is getting from them is nothing but sex. Also I looked at the fact that she goes to the club every Friday and Saturday. She is in at nine o'clock sharp and never leaves until the place close. How is it possible for a woman to be around so many single guys, but still remains single herself? You have to really observe people and read between the lines. The reason she doesn't have a man is because she's to busy lusting after all of them. What's more disturbing is she doesn't even see anything wrong with her approach. She believes she can't find a man because all of them are dogs. In transition, she can't find a man because she is the dog. Understand the majority of lusters will stay in denial to the end. That's why it's extremely hard to expose a luster by giving them the color code test because their answers won't hold true to their natural self. If I were to give her the test, the results would display a whole different person. That's because most people choose to hear good things about them selves rather than hear the truth. This goes back to why you must be true to yourself when going through this phase. That's the only way to find out what's right for you. You can lie to everyone else, but you can't lie to yourself. Accept yourself for who you truly are and you will find your place in this game of love or lust.

# CHAPTER 12:
# LOOK PAST WHAT YOU CAN SEE

Now that we have accepted ourselves we can start our path to find love. We first need to reprogram the way we look at others by wiping away all the stereotypes we see. Things like beauty, wealth, and race must become a thing of the past. America teaches us that beauty is measured by perfection. They unconsciously tell us beauty is a face with no scars, blemishes, and pimples. They teach us that beauty is a slim tight body with no fat or flaws. Beauty should be judged on a combination of the body and the personality. If you simply judge by the body what happens when that body starts to age. Will you still see your wife as that beautiful dame or will you see a woman, who once was a beautiful dame. See one thing about the personality is that its original and it doesn't change. It has the ability to make you laugh, and also make you cry. Most of all it has the ability to make you love, and that is what makes it beautiful. It's a shame most people don't allow them selves to see such a thing. Please look past the body and try to look for what you can't see. Don't let things like wealth and race stop you from defining a person? I understand some people are just comfortable with their own ethnic group. It's no problem with feeling that way. Just don't let the stereotypes of America decide your life. If we were color blind we would be forced to see people all the same, but unfortunately it doesn't work like that. Consequently, that doesn't mean you can't reprogram yourself to see like that. I will give you an example of what I mean. I have a friend named Larry who is black but his fiancé is white. Before they got together they both only dated within their own race. I will tell you the story of how they met and fell in love. While driving to work in the middle of Chicago's brutal winter, Larry spotted a car on the side of the road. He immediately got out and trampled through the thick snow to see who was in the vehicle. He noticed a woman inside by herself and asked her did she need help. The woman constantly rejected his help and stated she has help on the way. Larry nice and respectfully insisted on waiting with her until helped arrive. She steady declined saying she will be okay. Larry kind of figured it will take the help some while to come in the rough condition. He also noticed she was a little uncomfortable with him but he still wanted to help. So he ran to the trunk of his car and pulled out a heating blanket and jumper cables. He begged her to please take the blanket and warm up while he jump start the car. The woman cautiously took the blanket from Larry as she watched him closely. Larry jumped the car and told her to turn the heat on. He than reached in his car and pulled out a hot cup of freshly brewed coffee in a mug. He walked to the window and extended his arm to the woman. She paused for a second or two, than slowly grabbed the mug. Help soon arrived and they pulled her out of the ditch. Larry proceeded to get in his car and take off before being stopped by the woman. She apologized for her behavior and the way she reacted to his kindness. She emitted to being scared of him because he was African American. Two years later they are engaged and happy as can be. We must erase all the stereotypes that cloud our vision. I think everyone should be given a fair chance to prove themselves. The problem is we base what we know off of what we can see, instead of what can feel. Therefore, we unconsciously stop ourselves from ever getting to know someone we may really like.

# CHAPTER 13:
# AQUIRING THE CHEMISTRY FOR LOVE

Now that we now have reprogrammed our vision we can see clearly now. Let's say you have been observing this friend of yours for a little time now and you want to make it official. The both of you have been straight forward and honest with each other from the beginning. Understand the ways to achieve this chemistry is to be straight forward, honest, and assertive. These are the key elements to unlocking the chemistry for love. What you want to focus on now is being straight forward with any and every situation that arises. So now you go out on a serious date to see the level of chemistry you can build with them. This is where you want to flip back to chapter 3 so you can pin point a disaster. Focus on the conversation and what comes out there mouth. If you're dealing with a woman make sure you observe any repeated remarks revolving around materialistic things. It's nothing wrong with her inquiring about your career and goals. But the minute the conversation gets to personal you want to redirect it. If she starts to ask how much you make and do you spoil your women. Understand she is a materialistic luster, otherwise known as a gold digger. First, you should never ask a person how much money they make. Second, a person's money should not be the fruit of the conversation while trying to get to know a person. I'll give you an example and tell you a story of how I once met this girl at work. I worked at a call center checking in parolees for the state of Illinois. It was all right money but I was still living paycheck to paycheck at home with my mom. This girl was beautiful and had a joking personality like mine. We would always stop and talk why we was in the hallways everyday. I got her number and we talked on the phone for hours. I really thought I was on to something sincere. But I noticed after telling her my real financial state, slowly but surely she drifted off. I didn't hear from her too much, and the phone calls started to fade. I thought I had to say or do something wrong for such a thing to happen. I mean why she would even go through the trouble of calling, if she didn't want to be bothered. Suddenly like the switch of a light bulb it dawned on me. See we could dress comfortable at work with a plain shirt and jeans, but I enjoyed coming to work a little professional. I would usually wear a button down shirt with a blazer and some nice jeans because it made me feel better. I remember getting compliments from everybody like, "you look like a business man." Someone also had told me it looks like I had money, but we both new the truth. I started to put two and two together and I remember what she told me on the phone one time. She told me she is about her money. In fact, I remember her repeatedly telling me she only deals with people on her level. Now even though she didn't say it directly to me, I believe it was an indirect comment made to me. I guess she based her opinion on me from what I was wearing to work. But when the truth came out, I wasn't on her level. See it could have been chemistry developed between us, but it wasn't picked up. The energy she was applying wasn't equivalent to mine. Therefore, no chemistry was ever created, just a small spark that soon faded away. This also goes back into looking past what you can see. Now if you're dealing with a man, pay close attention to his eye contact, and the flow of his conversation. Make sure the both of you are giving feedback and focus on his eye contact. But in your case everything went find and he is paying attention to you. Okay now that everything is going okay you have acquired something. You have now acquired chemistry from being honest and straight forward. Understand chemistry is the energy that creates love. But both parties must project and observe this energy for love to be created. You can project such energy to me, but if I'm not focused on you it will bounce back to you. That means the possibility of us having chemistry is dead. Also if what you projected is falsehood or full of lies, if I was to absorb that energy we will have a lustful relationship. It's not from the heart, so we will have an infatuation instead of love. Understand you get out of a relationship exactly what you put in.

# CHAPTER 14:
# WHEN TO EXPLORE THE SEXUAL CHEMISTRY LEVEL

All right everything is now going just like you planned and you have acquired the chemistry for love. The chemistry level is very high from both ends and you know this is not an infatuation. You know because the energy you projected was sincere, honest, and not lustful. Chemistry has always been the most intriguing topic. It's something that can't be seen, measured, or predicted. It's the one thing that's so hard to find. What's even harder is when to react on it. Everybody wonders when it is the correct time to sexually explore. I don't think it's a necessary or certified time when you should put out. It all relies on the couple on how natural their chemistry flows. Now depending on what color your dealing with the night can end several different ways. We know you're not dealing with a yellow luster because you have observed this person and they have passed the disaster test. But if they were you would have ended the night early, due to you shutting down repeated tips towards sex or materialistic things. Unless, you were a luster yourself than you probably would have made lust with each other. But in this case you are not so you sent the trash home. Now if you're dealing with a yellow peacekeeper it's different. Understand peacekeepers fall hard, and at times they can't level their emotions. Therefore, if you were a peacekeeper also it would be a perfect match. It will be a lot of heated and confusing moments. But the both of you move fast so you don't have to worry about losing each other. Let's switch it up and say tonight you are a white. That would mean you may want to take it slow, being that you are dealing with a yellow. Most whites don't like to move drastically fast, and they don't like to be smothered. If a peacekeepers emotions get out of control to early in the whole process. Most whites will bag up because they hate unorganized emotions. So you may want to wait and take it slow with them. Now let's say you're dealing with a red color. Most likely since you followed the right patterns, you have showed them true sincere feelings. For most reds they have never experienced the real thing. They will be able to handle that sexual chemistry; in fact they have the possibility of being some of the most passionate lovers. Now if you are a red yourself you have to be very careful. See most reds still struggle with trust and pride factors. They often at times hold back and get irritated with the ways of love. They usually need someone as strong as a blue or white to redirect their focus. What if both parties are reds, who will redirect those emotions to enforce the trust? So it would be extremely hard trying to get through arguments and disagreements, but it's possible. Now let's say you're dealing with a white tonight. They are very capable of sexual chemistry, but the problem would rely on what color you are. If you are a luster you will get shutdown immediately. You won't get a chance to get anything over on a white. Now if you are a red dealing with a white everything will be okay. Reds will have to be strong to deal with a white because whites are strong spirited. Now let's say you are dealing with a blue, yes today is your lucky day. In a situation with a blue it will definitely be okay to progress through sexual chemistry. Blues highly understand chemistry and can control their emotions extremely well. They know the twist and turns of dealing with love in relationships. Now we very well know at this point that luster's are the opposite of the blues so that's out of the question. Let's say you are a red, that's an interesting match to make with a blue. The sexual chemistry will be spontaneous, due to reds being welcomed for the first time to raw pure love. Now if you are a peacekeeper, this will be a very debating relationship. That's because blues are in control of their emotions, and peacekeepers are the exact opposite. So there will always be that on going battle of reasoning over right and wrong. Now what would happen if you were white, things would be very interesting. See most whites love a challenge, and enjoy a party who can keep up on a mental level. Blues are the perfect breed who can satisfy and yet surpass these obstacles. Blues is the only color that can captivate a white's emotions and leave them shaken up. They are the natural lovers who can create that strong love that most whites don't believe in. So let's say it is your lucky day and you have found a blue. The both of you have played by the rules and now you have made it to love.

# CHAPTER 15:
# WELCOME TO LOVE

Finally we have arrived to that point we have been chasing our whole lives. That myth that true love doesn't exist, does not apply to us anymore. We are on another plain where physical insecurities and stereotypes can't hurt. We are one of the very few who has such a thing. Consequently, we have a very big problem we have to deal with for the rest of our lives. We have to do something much harder than finding love, and that's keeping it. We have to come across all the rest of the active players in the game, including the lusters. Everybody wants what we have and now we are the admired ones. The hunter has just become the hunted and now is the time to be on guard. Liars will come out to deceive us and whisper if you let them. Jealous and envy one's will set out to divide us if you allow them. Luster's will crawl out to destroy our love with every little bit of life inside of them. These are very crucial times where one small mistake can erase a lifetime of happiness.

# CHAPTER 16:
# KEEPING LOVE

Now we have to fight to keep our love active and strong so we never get divided. Most of the key elements are simply reapplying the same efforts we took to get here. In transition, there are three major keys we must follow to maintain love. We must be passionate, stay honest, and have faith in each other. Now if all three of these elements stay surfaced, life will be enjoyable to the end of your days. You can't apply energy to two and leave the other vacant. This here is a package deal, and there will be serious struggles if these laws are broken. Now let's start with keeping the love we have active and passionate. I can't stress to you how important it is to be spontaneous with your partner. Most couple's problems arise when they get to comfortable with each other after being together for so long. You don't do most of the things you did when you first met, and those simple compliments go away. Those little compliments go along way, and actually enhance one's confidence. Remember everything counts when you progress further and further into your relationship. You do not want to get comfortable with doing the same thing the same way. Try to be spontaneous and different with your approach in every situation. Flirt a little and be creative besides jumping straight into bed. Maybe even create an erotic theme in the house. Dem the lights, spread rose pedals over the floor, and light scented candles all over the house. You want to focus on everything around the actual moment before arriving to it. Be spontaneous like going out somewhere you usually never go, be open to try new things. Most of the time when that comfort sets in, it draws a wedge between you. Now here comes the division from all angles tearing and prying its way in. This usually leads to the curiosity in others and can often lead to infidelity. You do not want to give any room for that to happen. It's not anything drastically different about what you may see in others. It's just that whenever one is subjected to the same routine for so long, everything around them seems interesting. So remember to stay active and spontaneous and everything will be okay. Also you have to be passionate about yourself too. You can't get comfortable and let yourself physically slip away to the point of no return. Understand you still have to keep yourself up to pardon at all times. I'm not talking about gaining a couple of pounds or small insignificant things. I'm talking about letting your spouse see you in the same house clothes everyday. Or not grooming yourself until you have to attend a. public meeting. These things matter because your spouse gets use to you looking like crap. You don't want that feeling to set in on you because your spouse will unconsciously start looking somewhere else. Your spouse may not physically go out to find someone, but will spot a characteristic in another person without trying. That's what I mean by unconsciously looking else where. I have seen this many times before and I believe you have also seen something similar. You know of this too, or you are experiencing this now as you read. Understand this type of relationship is also a lustful one, due from two people catering to a relationship where there hearts are not in it. That goes back to the ending fact that lust can only end in hurt. So remember to keep the passion going and everything will be okay.

# CHAPTER 17:
# STAY HONEST

I believe the word honest is used so much today that it has also lost its meaning. You must understand that confining within your love is of great importance. You want to be able to tell the truth at all times, no matter how bad it will hurt them. Hiding and lying will only distance you from each other. How I see it, I want you to be able to tell me anything. I want to know your worst fears and your greatest desires. If I push you away, that will only result in you turning to someone else. I want you to be my lover and I also my best friend. Always say what's on your mind and speak on how you feel. Being secretive creates an invisible force field that brings division between you. Now when I was with the mother of my child, we had this same problem. In fact, there were plenty of times when I tried to tell her about my dreams, and she wouldn't pay attention. I would tell her how I was gone be a writer, and she would laugh or give me a silly look. She didn't believe in me and was not sincere when I tried to discuss these things with her. So in return I talked to other girls who actually took the time to listen and actually gave me feedback. We never were one with each other because we never confined to one another. In transition, not being honest broke up all the trust that we ever had.

# CHAPTER 18:

# THE ABSENTY OF TRUST

Trust is the number one reason why most relationships today struggle to make it and often fail. Please understand if you don't have trust, you don't have anything at all. In fact, the majority of people I interviewed told me they do not trust their spouse. Even though they remain together, they still do not trust them and find it difficult to believe them. I asked them what made them stay and cater to that type of relationship. Some told me they need cold hard evidence, like catching their spouse in the act of cheating. Others told me they can't find anything better so they just deal with what they got. Now if you look deeper into both of those situations, they are just explosions waiting to happen. They are both lustful situations because the heart isn't in the relationship anymore. Not having trust in your spouse leads to insecurity issues. These issues bring about strong feelings of jealousy and envy. That's when the arguing starts from missed phone calls and late appearances. Understand when you don't have trust, you will unconsciously make something out of nothing. Even if for that one time your spouse is telling the truth, you still won't believe them. Once upon a time I fell in love with a woman who until this day, still causes my heart to skip a beat. We broke up because she accused me of cheating. Now at the time she was hurt because she really thought I cheated, but in all actuality I did not commit any of the things she suggested. She kept screaming at me telling me to confess to the rumors. After an hour of being drilled I just complied with whatever she was saying. I told her if she believes in those rumors than maybe I did cheat on her. I should have understood that she was emotionally affected at the time. It was wrong of me to act in a negative way, when I should have waited until she calmed down. Instead I told her I did do it, and I paid dearly for that. Understand she was very sincere with her emotions, and she felt hurt so she was very angry. If I knew what I knew now, I would have allowed her time to calm down. After that she was convinced I cheated, and that was it for us. It's funny how it takes a lifetime to gain a person's trust, but it takes only a second to lose it. When you lose a person's trust you lose something that is nearly impossible to replace. I really loved that girl; in fact she was the only blue I ever ran into. See I can't explain what made me love her so much. When I think of her I don't think of any sexual acts. I'm comforted with her by holding her hand or simply just spending time with her. When I was around her I wasn't focused on having sex with her. That was actually the last thing on my mind when I gazed into her eyes. I was satisfied with her just enjoying my company. All women can't captivate a man that way. She actually shut down all my sexual thinking, and made me analyze her with my heart. Only one other girl made me see her for her and that was Siyo. But that's in the past now so the show must move on. You sincerely have to trust your spouse to survive your relationship. Consequently, in order to trust one, you must first have faith in them.

# CHAPTER 19:
# FACT OR FAITH

Most people struggle so hard to believe in something that they can't see. That's because without trust you can't have faith in a person. How can you have faith in something you don't believe in? Most people trust in what they can see, which is the facts. So in all actually they really don't trust in their spouse, but in how the facts add up. Let me give you a prime example of what I'm trying to say. I dealt with this insecure girl for a short time. It all came to an end when our trust was put to the test. One morning while going to work a strong thunderstorm hit. It created a power outage through the whole town. In fact, it even caused our cell phones to lose signals. So now I can't contact her until I get home. While at work my cousin walked up to my job to borrow my car. I told him he can borrow it if he brings it back before I get off. So he agreed and he took off on his way. Now in the meantime my girl was at home by herself. She had been trying to call me but she couldn't get through. So she decided to drive up to my job to make sure everything was okay. The problem was she didn't see my car in the parking lot, so she turned around thinking I wasn't there. Later on I get home and she is sitting on the couch with a devilish look. I thought something happen so I asked her what the matter is. She started screaming to the top of her voice, repeatedly asking where I have been. I told her I was at work, and I came straight home. She asked where my car was and I told her my cousin had it. Now let's analyze this whole situation for a second. If she trusted me with her faith we would have not had to argue. She would have simply asked me where my car was, and I would have told her. There would have been no problems after that. In transition, her trust in me was based off of facts. If she would have come inside and physically saw me, everything would have been okay. But she didn't see me, so now she had to go on her faith to believe me. She didn't have trust in faith, she had trust in facts. If your going to be committed than be sole fully committed to the one you're with. Give no room for people to whisper in your ear and tell you what they saw. If outsider's see any opening to exploit your love they will. Before you accept what strangers say you ask your spouse first. They deserve that much; they deserve a fair chance to give their side of the story. It's a shame that most of our faith in relationships today is based on what we can see. But this is one ongoing battle we will one day have to overcome.

# CHAPTER 20:
# NO MORE EXSCUSES

We have now passed the tide that threatened are every move of finding love. We now understand that certain people react certain ways because we are all color-coded. We understand there are sincere steps that must be followed to achieve true love. We know we must accept ourselves, be assertive, and be passionate to maintain our love. We know you have to be honest to gain trust, and we must trust with our faith. You now have all the tools to find, acquire, and keep love. While rapping this up I would like to let you know what brought me to this stage. See I am one of those true blues I have been telling you about. I noticed I have always looked at love more sincerely than others. In fact most girls my age always said I was too serious. That's probably why I always dealt with girls much older than me. I must give thanks to the mother of my child for simply being her. See I broke it off because I knew we weren't going about it right. In fact, I knew we had not been sincere; I knew we were simply lusting. So a couple weeks after I broke it off, I found out one of my best friend's was with her. I was so angered that my friend would go behind my back. I was also angry at her but not as much as I was at him. I felt he could have been a man and told me up front what was going on. Try to understand the key word angered. See I wasn't hurt or heartbroken I was mad and frustrated. It was more of a pride issue for me. It didn't affect me at all like losing my first love I talked about. That because what we endured was a lustful situation. Maybe at the beginning it was sincere but at that moment it wasn't. She was talking to other guys and I reacted by talking to other girls. That's what you call fighting fire with fire, but indeed that is the wrong way. I should have simply ended the relationship then, instead of trying to continue knowing we were not sincere with each other anymore. Actually most people today are engaged in relationships today where they know their sincerity is gone. Me being a blue I understood that it wasn't love, than I quickly recuperated from it. I analyzed all the right and wrongs about the situation.

Understand this lustful situation was my entire fault. Being that I was aware of what was to come from enduring a lustful relationship, that means I was the more responsible one. Whenever you are in control of a situation you are therefore the leader. So by all means if you lead in a lustful way, you will suffer lustful consequences. In transition, I have been led down this very road I'm at now. I want to thank everyone who took the time to read this guide. I sincerely believe if these rules are followed you will definitely be able to pin point love from lust. Understand that we are all made of love, and GOD is love.

Thank you for giving me your time. In return I would like to share with you the actual poem LOVE OR LUST.

WHAT IS IT REALLY TO SAY EXCEPT FOR THE FACT THAT LOVE HAS DIED? CUPID HAS RETREATED BACK TO THE PITS OF THE EARTH WHERE ONLY DARKNESS CAN SEE HIM. SO MANY HAS CLAIMED TO LOVE HIM AND HONORED HIS PRESENCE. BUT IN ALL ACTUALLY THEY DENIED, USED, AND ABUSED THE ONLY THING THAT MADE US, US. THE ONLY THING THAT MADE OUR HEARTS SMILE. THE ONLY THING THAT WAS WORTH DIEING FOR. SO NOW WE SCATTER AROUND THIS EARTH LUSTING WITHOUT CAUSE. TAKE YOUR CHANCES ON YOUR OWN, LOVE YOUR OWN WAY. AS FOR ME, I AM A LOVER SO I REQUIRE THE REAL THING. BUT IF YOU DO SO TOO, THAN GRAB CUPID WINGS AND ESCAPE WITH ME. FOR WE WILL FLY TO THE END OF THE EARTH AND I WILL FOREVER SHOW YOU TRUE LOVE. IF NOT, STAY HERE AND EXCEPT THIS DEGRADING EMOTION YOU CALL LOVE. AND WHEN YOU REALIZE LOVE IS GONE, COME FIND ME AT THE END OF THE SUNSET. THERE WILL I LOVE YOU UNTIL THE STARS FALL FROM THE SKIES. WHO AM I, I AM LOVE.

www.ingramcontent.com/pod-product-compliance
Lightning Source LLC
Chambersburg PA
CBHW070842310526
45793CB00011B/500